D1228702

C L A S S I C
StoryTellers

EDGAR ALLAN POE

P.O. Box 196
Hockessin, Delaware 19707

Titles in the Series

Judy Blume

Stephen Crane

F. Scott Fitzgerald

Ernest Hemingway

Jack London

Katherine Paterson

Edgar Allan Poe

John Steinbeck

Harriet Beecher Stowe

Mildred Taylor

Mark Twain

E. B. White

CLASSIC
StoryTellers

EDGAR ALLAN POE

Jim Whiting

Mitchell Lane
PUBLISHERS

Printing 1   2   3   4   5   6   7   8
Library of Congress Cataloging-in-Publication Data
Whiting, Jim, 1943-
    Edgar Allan Poe / by Jim Whiting.
        p. cm — (Classic storytellers)
    Includes bibliographical references and index.
    ISBN 1-58415-373-3 (lib. bdg.)
1. Poe, Edgar Allan, 1809-1849—Juvenile literature. 2. Authors, American—19th century —Biography—Juvenile literature. I. Title. II. Series.
PS2631.W49 2005
818'.309—dc22
                                       2005004244

ABOUT THE AUTHOR: Jim Whiting has been a remarkably versatile and accomplished journalist, writer, editor and photographer for more than 30 years. A voracious reader since early childhood, Mr. Whiting has written and edited about 200 non-fiction children's books. His subjects range from authors to zoologists and include contemporary pop icons and classical musicians, saints and scientists, emperors and explorers. Representative titles include *The Life and Times of Franz Liszt, The Life and Times of Julius Caesar, Charles Schulz* and *Juan Ponce de Leon.*

    Other career highlights are a lengthy stint publishing *Northwest Runner,* the first piece of original fiction to appear in *Runners World* magazine, hundreds of descriptions and venue photographs for *America Online,* e-commerce product writing, sports editor for the *Bainbridge Island Review,* light verse in a number of magazines and acting as the official photographer for the *Antarctica Marathon.*

    He lives in Washington state with his wife and two teenage sons.

PUBLISHER'S NOTE: This story is based on the author's extensive research, which he believes to be accurate. Documentation of such research is contained on page 46-47.

    The internet sites referenced herein were active as of the publication date. Due to the fleeting nature of some web sites, we cannot guarantee they will all be active when you are reading this book.

Contents

EDGAR ALLAN POE

Jim Whiting

*For Your Information

This photo of Edgar Allan Poe was taken in November, 1848. At the time he was trying to convince a woman he barely knew to marry him. It was an especially low point in his life. The image clearly shows his unhappiness.

Chapter 1

A GRUESOME CRIME

Residents of a neighborhood in Paris, France, are awakened early one morning by a series of hideous screams that come from the top floor of one of the houses. The alarmed neighbors race to the house. They pound on the front door. When no one lets them in, they pry the door open. As they rush up the stairs, they hear two angry voices shouting at each other. One is clearly French. The other speaks in a language that no one can identify. By the time the neighbors reach the top floor, the voices have fallen silent. They rush from room to room, but everything seems in order. When they try to enter a large room at the rear of the house, the door is locked—from the inside, they discover after breaking it down when there is no response to their knocking.

Inside the room, all is chaos. Chunks of broken furniture are everywhere. A chest of drawers has been yanked open and some of the clothes thrown onto the floor. A razor smeared with blood lies on a chair. There are several thick, bloody clumps of gray hair, which appear to have been torn out by the roots.

By this time the neighbors are feeling pretty nervous. They notice a large pile of soot in the middle of the fireplace. One of them looks up into the chimney and recoils in horror. A young woman has been thrust feet-first into the chimney. When her lifeless body is pulled down, the cause of death is obvious. Large bruises on her throat indicate that she has been strangled by a pair of very powerful hands.

A few minutes later, there is an even more gruesome discovery. The young woman's mother is lying in a small courtyard behind the building. She has been savagely mutilated. Many of her bones are broken, and bruises cover her entire body. Her throat has been slashed so badly that her head falls off when the residents pick up the corpse.

The police are summoned. Their investigation reveals that the two women lived quietly and had no known enemies. They further observe that a great deal of money is lying in plain sight in the apartment. Therefore, the most obvious possible motives for such a ghastly crime—revenge and robbery—can't explain it. Nor can the police figure out how the culprits escaped. They certainly didn't come down the steps while the neighbors were going up, and there are no other sets of stairs they could have used. A trapdoor leading to the roof is nailed shut. So are the windows that overlook the courtyard. Even if the killers went out through one of those windows, it is more than a forty-foot drop onto hard cobblestones. The police are baffled.

This is the mystery that lies at the heart of "The Murders in the Rue Morgue," a short story by Edgar Allan Poe. The story, published in 1841, is one of Poe's best-known works. It is also one of his most important. It was the first story in which a detective solves a mystery. In fact, the word *detective* dates from about this time.

With the police investigation at a standstill, a man named Auguste Dupin (pronounced oh-GOOST doo-PAN) becomes interested in the crime. Dupin has many similarities to Poe, his creator. He is very intelligent. He has a keenly analytic mind. He enjoys solving puzzles—especially ones that seem impossible to most people.

Near the beginning of the story, Dupin reveals these qualities when he and a friend—the narrator of the story—are walking along a street in Paris. Neither man has said a word for at least fifteen minutes. Suddenly Dupin makes a comment showing that he has apparently read his friend's mind. He says exactly what his friend has just been thinking. Amazed, the friend asks for an explanation. Dupin is happy to oblige. He explains that he has been carefully observing him—facial expressions, the direction in which he looks, even his posture. These observations form the basis for the comment.

Soon after this demonstration of his superior mental gifts, Dupin and his friend hear about the crime in the Rue Morgue. They read that the police have made an arrest. It is the bank clerk who delivered the money to the two women several days earlier. There is no solid evidence against the man, but the brutal nature of the crime has put a lot of pressure on the police to find the killer.

Dupin is acquainted with the clerk, who once did a favor for him. Even though he has no connection with the police force, Dupin decides to join the investigation. He knows a high-ranking police official. He asks this official for permission to view the crime scene. It is granted. Dupin and his friend spend several hours there. On their way home, Dupin makes a quick stop at one of the local newspapers. He places an ad in a newspaper's lost-and-found section. He doesn't explain why he does this.

The following day, Dupin asks his friend if he had noticed anything peculiar the previous day during their examination of the crime scene. The friend replies that he hadn't. Dupin then casually announces that he has solved the crime. In the next breath, he tells his astonished friend that someone who is directly connected with the awful event will shortly appear because of the ad he placed in the newspaper. He takes out two pistols. He puts one in his pocket and hands the other one to his friend. Then he explains his reasoning.

The two men settle into their easy chairs. Soon there is a knock on the door.

"Please enter," says Dupin.

The door opens. When he sees the person who enters the room, Dupin knows that his reasoning has been correct. The killer is . . .

"The Murders in the Rue Morgue" paved the way for such fictional detective heroes as Sherlock Holmes, Agatha Christie's Hercule Poirot, and the legion of contemporary sleuths. Thousands of mystery novels are published every year. They are one of the most popular types of reading, selling millions of copies.

In 1907, Arthur Conan Doyle, the creator of Sherlock Holmes, wrote, "If every man who receives a cheque [check] for a story which owes its springs to Poe were to pay tithe to a monument for the master, he would have a pyramid as big as that of Cheops."[1] With the explosive growth of mystery stories since then, the size of that monument would now be far larger than a single pyramid.

Some mystery writers even incorporate Poe into their plots. For example, a prominent feature of Michael Connelly's 1996 novel *The Poet* is fake suicide notes, each of which quotes some lines from Poe's poetry.

Many modern mystery writers continue to use plot devices that Poe pioneered. One is the locked room. Another involves a somewhat dim-witted sidekick, whose questions allow the detective to demonstrate his or her cleverness. Official law enforcement personnel are frequently portrayed as bumblers who resent the superior crime-solving powers of the stories' heroes and heroines.

Another characteristic of a detective story is that the mystery is solved at the end. But Edgar Allan Poe's own story doesn't have such a tidy conclusion. While nearly all of the details of his life are well known, the circumstances of his death remain shrouded in mystery. Until a real-life Auguste Dupin comes along, they are likely to remain so.

FYInfo

A Real-Life Mystery Story

"The Murders in the Rue Morgue" was published in April 1841. Three months later, Poe heard the shocking details of a real murder. A group of men walking along the banks of the Hudson River in New Jersey discovered the body of a young woman floating in the river.

The woman was Mary Cecilia Rogers. She had told her boyfriend that she was going to visit her aunt. She never arrived. The case normally wouldn't have attracted much attention, but Mary worked at the front counter of a cigar store in an area that housed numerous newspapers. Many reporters knew her personally. They also knew that her youth, beauty, and tragic end would help sell newspapers. Her case became front-page news. The coverage of every detail and every possible lead was similar to the publicity given to the Nicole Simpson/Ronald Goldman and Laci Peterson murder cases.

At first, police believed Rogers had been assaulted by a gang of several men. Suspicion also fell on her boyfriend, Daniel Payne, and some previous boyfriends. But no one was arrested. Payne committed suicide a few months later. Because he had a solid alibi, people believed that grief was the reason he took his own life.

A year later, a woman named Frederica Loss made a deathbed confession. Loss, who ran a boarding-

O. J. Simpson was a suspect in a modern day mystery murder.

house, claimed that there had been no murder. Instead, Mary had come to her establishment to have an abortion. Complications set in, and Mary died on the operating table. Loss and her sons helped the man who performed the abortion make it appear that Mary had been murdered.

Some people were skeptical. They said that Loss was barely conscious at the time and may have been hallucinating. They also said that her story didn't account for all the details of the crime. The case remains unofficially unsolved.

Poe decided to use the Rogers case as another example of Auguste Dupin's crime-solving ability. He changed Mary's name and moved the crime scene to the Seine River in Paris. Entitled "The Mystery of Marie Rogêt," the story was published in 1842.

This illustration shows Boston during the Colonial Era. Then as now, the city was one of the most important in America. It probably looked much the same when Edgar Poe was born several decades later.

Chapter 2

ACTING OUT HIS PART

Edgar Poe was born in Boston, Massachusetts, on January 19, 1809. His parents, David Poe and Elizabeth Hopkins Poe, were both actors. Edgar was the couple's second child. He joined his brother, Henry, who had been born in 1807. A third child, Rosalie, was born in 1810.

In that era, actors didn't make much money. To earn enough to support themselves, they constantly had to travel between numerous cities. With their growing family, David and Elizabeth had to work even harder.

Fortunately, Elizabeth was a gifted and popular actress. She began her stage career at the age of nine. According to contemporary accounts, she played nearly 300 roles during her career. Her performances were acclaimed by both audiences and critics. David Poe had been a law student when he attended one of her performances. He fell in love with her. He dropped out of law school and became an actor so that he could be with her. He was not very good, and his performances were often criticized. He began quarreling with Elizabeth and drank heavily.

Not long after Rosalie's birth, David Poe abandoned his family. He may have been jealous of the far better reviews that his wife received for her acting. He also may have felt burdened by the pressures of a growing family. The rest of his family disapproved of his decision to become an actor and refused to help him financially. It is believed that he died of tuberculosis not long after his disappearance.

To ease the burden of being a single mother, Elizabeth sent Henry to live with relatives. It was still a struggle to support herself and her other two children. Perhaps exhausted by that struggle, Elizabeth contracted tuberculosis in the fall of 1811. She gave her final performance in Richmond, Virginia, in mid-October. Because of her popularity, her illness attracted a great deal of attention. A number of fans brought food for her and her children, and tried to ease her suffering. Despite their best efforts, she died two months later. She was only twenty-four.

Her death almost certainly made a strong impression on her sensitive son, who was just a month away from his third birthday. Describing her at her wake, Poe biographer Wolf Mankowitz observes, "The small fairy-like figure of his mother wearing her best gown, her face white as wax after the hectic color of her last days, illuminated by candles, an ultimate dream-lady deep in her mysterious sleep, remained one of the most haunting images of Poe's childhood."[1]

Elizabeth Poe left behind two orphans. The children were fortunate to be quickly adopted. Edgar's new parents were John and Frances Allan of Richmond, who had no children of their own. They had attended many of Elizabeth's performances, and Frances Allan was one of the women who had helped Elizabeth during her final illness. Frances must have felt a special kinship with Edgar, because she had also been an orphan. She was warm and affectionate toward the little boy.

Although the Allans treated Edgar as if he were their son, they never legally adopted him. They did, however, give him their last name. From then on, he would be known as Edgar Allan Poe. They also gave him much more stability. John Allan was a tobacco and dry-goods merchant who had a steady income from his business. As a result, Edgar lived in a large house rather than a series of tiny apartments. He dressed in good clothing. He ate well. He had playmates and pets. He went with the Allans on vacations to fashionable resorts. He had a personal tutor, then began attending a highly regarded private school.

He also demonstrated that he had inherited his mother's acting ability. "[The Allans] were fond of exhibiting his precocious talents to their evening guests; and Edgar's retentive memory enabled him to learn and recite the most moving and beautiful passages of English poetry," writes biographer Jeffrey Meyers. "He was encouraged to stand on the dining-room table in his stockinged feet and toast the health of the ladies with a glass of sweetened wine."[2]

During the first years of Edgar's life, tensions were growing between the United States and Great Britain. Finally, open warfare broke out in the War of 1812. When the conflict ended early in 1815, John Allan decided to take advantage of the renewed trade between the two countries by opening an office in London. He took his wife and Edgar with him. Even though the open-ocean voyage lasted for more than a month and must have included some rough seas, six-year-old Edgar boasted that he was never scared.

After visiting relatives in Allan's native Scotland, the family settled in London. Edgar attended two boarding schools. The first one was a local school in Chelsea, a district in London. The second was a more advanced school in the village of Stoke-Newington, just north of London. By all reports, Edgar did well in the two schools. He learned Latin, French, and history. He read Shakespeare and other noted English authors. He also had the opportunity to read the works of such prominent poets as Percy Bysshe Shelley and Johann Wolfgang von Goethe. These poets were associated with the romantic movement, which emphasized the importance of feelings and the natural world.

Poe's rapid progress must have been gratifying to John Allan, who had little formal education of his own. Allan willingly paid the substantial cost of a good education for Edgar.

Unfortunately, the market for tobacco collapsed in 1819, and it was no longer profitable for the firm to maintain the London branch. The following year the Allans returned to the United States. For John Allan, it was a somewhat difficult time because of the uncertain prospects for his business. For his foster son, it may have been the happiest period of his life. One reason was that Allan continued to support Edgar's education even though it had become a financial hardship. Edgar went to school at Joseph H. Clarke's academy. He rewarded Allan's support by ranking among the best students in his class. One of his accomplishments was reading Homer's epic poems *The Iliad* and *The Odyssey* in the original ancient Greek. He was also starting to write poetry and other types of literature.

In spite of all his success in school, and the advantages that living with the Allans had given him, there was one handicap Edgar could never overcome. His birth parents had been actors. No matter how much audiences applauded them while they were onstage, it was an entirely different matter when they weren't performing. Unlike the present day, when good actors (and even some who aren't very good) are high-profile celebrities, actors in Edgar's era had a dubious reputation. This was especially true in the South, where many wealthy people regarded themselves as aristocrats, and actors as far beneath them.

As one of Edgar's classmates noted, "It was known that his parents had been players [actors], and that he was dependent upon the bounty that is bestowed upon an adopted son. All this had the effect of making the boys decline his leadership; and on looking back on it since, I fancy it gave him a fierceness he would otherwise not have had."[3]

As we might say today, Edgar probably had a chip on his shoulder. The "fierceness" his classmate mentioned found several physical outlets. Edgar was more than just a bookworm. He often challenged classmates to footraces, boxing matches, and other forms of athletic competition. Once he swam six miles in the James River against an incoming tide. He long-jumped nearly 20 feet, an excellent mark even by today's standards. He also joined a group called the Morgan Junior Riflemen. The group formed part of an honor guard for Revolutionary War hero the Marquis de Lafayette during his visit in 1824.

Not long before Lafayette's visit, Edgar had developed a crush on Jane Stanard. She was the beautiful mother of one of his friends. To Edgar, Jane was the symbol of the perfect woman. She would be the inspiration for his poem "Helen." (Helen was the lovely woman whose abduction ignited the legendary Trojan War—an event still fresh in his mind from his reading of Homer.) It was therefore a profound shock when she suffered a brain tumor in 1824. She died after a brief period of insanity. Once again a beautiful woman to whom he was attached was gone. In the weeks after her death, he frequently visited her grave.

Up to this point, he and Allan—who had often boasted of Edgar's academic accomplishments—had gotten along well. With Jane Stanard's death, Edgar became more moody. Now fifteen, it is likely that he was also starting a period of typical teenage rebellion. He made Allan very upset one day when he went to a nearby plantation and shot a number of birds. On another occasion, he dressed up as a ghost and tried to frighten the members of a club. These antics embarrassed his foster father.

It didn't help that the monetary problems Allan's company faced were growing even worse. These problems threatened him with bankruptcy. In addition to financial ruin, bankruptcy would also bring humiliation in the status-conscious South. Meanwhile Allan, as a "self-made man," had trouble understanding his sensitive foster son. Edgar's grief over Jane Stanard's death would have been incomprehensible to him. As Allan complained in a letter, "The boy possesses not a Spark of affection for us not a particle of gratitude for all my care and kindness towards him."[4]

In the spring of the following year, Allan was having breakfast with a wealthy uncle, William Galt. As Allan and another man helped the uncle to an easy chair, the older man died before their very eyes. Galt was reputed to be Virginia's wealthiest man, and Allan received today's equivalent of several million dollars. His financial problems were over. He used the money to pay off his debts and buy a large mansion in Richmond. Edgar may have started dreaming of being in a similar situation himself at some point in the future.

FYInfo

Tuberculosis

Poe's parents were hardly alone in dying of tuberculosis. TB was the leading cause of death in that era. Some famous nineteenth-century victims were poet John Keats, novelist Robert Louis Stevenson, composer Frédéric Chopin, and most of the Brontë family—Charlotte Brontë wrote *Jane Eyre,* while Emily Brontë was the author of *Wuthering Heights.* Traces of the disease date back nearly 4,500 years to ancient Egypt, and it was well known to the classical Greeks.

The disease is very contagious. It thrives in the unsanitary conditions that have characterized most of human history. It usually attacks the lungs, though other organs can also be affected. Its main symptoms are severe coughing, weight loss, high fevers, and sweating.

Tuberculosis acquired many grim nicknames. One of them, "the captain of the men of death," reflects the high number of victims it claimed. It was also called "the white plague" because of the pale skin that was one of its characteristics. Another name was "consumption," because it seemed literally to consume the bodies of its victims as they wasted away.

In 1882, German doctor Robert Koch finally identified the cause. It

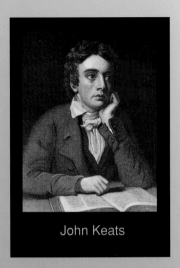

John Keats

was a form of bacteria, which he named *Mycobacterium tuberculosis.* Still, no cure was found for another half century. In 1943, American researcher Selman Waksman discovered streptomycin. This drug and several similar ones proved effective in combating the disease. However, tuberculosis bacteria are very hard to kill, so the treatment program can last for up to two years.

Even with modern drug therapy and heightened standards of cleanliness, tuberculosis hasn't gone away. More than 15,000 cases are reported in the United States annually, though most can be treated. In the rest of the world, it is estimated that upward of two million people die of tuberculosis every year. It remains a serious world health problem.

Thomas Jefferson was one of the most important of the United States' "Founding Fathers." He wrote the Declaration of Independence and served as the third president. Perhaps his most famous accomplishment as president was the Louisiana Purchase. It more than doubled the country's size.

Chapter 3

CADET POE

Edgar realized one immediate benefit from John Allan's new wealth. Now aged sixteen, he found himself welcome in many of Richmond's best homes. He began seeing a girl named Elmira Royster, who was a year younger than he was. Their romance developed quickly, and Elmira regarded herself as engaged to Edgar.

A few months later—in February 1826—Edgar entered the University of Virginia. The university was located in Charlottesville, about sixty miles from Richmond. It was the final major project of former president Thomas Jefferson and had been open for only a year. Some of the buildings still hadn't been completed.

The campus environment was rough. Many students fought with each other, attended cockfights, threw bricks at professors they didn't like, drank heavily, gambled for high stakes, and even carried pistols. When he wasn't joining his fellow students in some of these rowdy activities, Edgar studied languages—French, Greek, Italian, Latin, and Spanish.

Even though Allan was no longer worried about money, his feelings toward Edgar hadn't changed. He

One of Thomas Jefferson's final achievements was founding the University of Virginia (shown here). He designed the school's buildings and campus. Edgar Allan Poe was among the first students who attended the University. Today the school has about 20,000 students. Many people consider it to be the best public university in the country.

kept the young man on a very tight financial leash. Some commentators even suggest that Edgar didn't have enough money to buy essential items.

The situation came to a head at Christmas. Edgar had lost a great deal of money playing cards. It is possible that Edgar, who was much younger than most of his fellow students, was the victim of cheating by his more experienced colleagues. John Allan said he would not pay Edgar's gambling debts. He also refused to pay for any more schooling, which meant that Edgar couldn't return to his classes.

That wasn't the only shock. Edgar had sent many letters to Elmira, but she hadn't responded. He learned that her father had kept all of his letters from reaching her. Not unreasonably, Elmira believed that he no longer cared for her. She had become engaged to another young man. It is likely that she didn't really care for her husband. According to the later recollections of a friend, Elmira said, "I married another man, but the love of my life was Edgar Poe. I never loved anyone else."[1]

Edgar was forced to work for Allan, who paid him nothing for his services. It was a tense situation, and it couldn't last very long. Within a few months they had a violent argument. Allan ordered him to leave home.

With almost no money, Edgar made his way to Boston. He published a thin volume of poetry called *Tamerlane and Other Poems*. Hardly anyone paid attention. So few copies were printed, in fact, that the book is now extremely rare—and a collector's item. In the 1990s, one of the very few surviving copies of the book sold for almost $200,000.[2]

Edgar enlisted in the U.S. Army under the name of Edgar A. Perry, apparently to escape his creditors. It seems he had stopped drinking and became a good soldier. In less than two years he was promoted to sergeant major, the highest rank that an enlisted man could achieve. He began to think of attending the U.S. Military Academy at West Point, New York, so that he could become a commissioned officer. He needed John Allan's support. Somewhat to

Edgar's surprise, Allan agreed. But he also conveyed some unhappy news. Edgar hadn't written to Fanny Allan for two years. He learned that she was seriously ill. He rushed home, but she died just before he arrived.

While he was waiting to enter West Point, Poe published *Al Aaraaf, Tamerlane and Minor Poems,* his second book of poetry. It didn't do much better than its predecessor. In June 1830, he was finally admitted to West Point. At first, things went well. Edgar applied himself to the rigorous discipline of the academy. He also became popular among his fellow cadets, telling them stories about his many "adventures." These stories were false, but the cadets—most of whom were several years younger than he was—believed him. He also continued to write poetry.

It didn't take long for Edgar's life to fall apart. In October 1830, John Allan married Louisa Patterson. It seemed apparent that he wanted to have children of his own, who would become his heirs in place of Edgar. Allan was still very tight with money. Edgar realized that he was condemned to a life of poverty if he stayed in the army, because military pay was very low. Edgar wanted out. Just as he had needed Allan's consent to enter West Point, he needed it to leave. At first Allan hesitated to give it. He held out hope that Edgar could still be successful.

Allan soon changed his mind.

Just before entering the academy, Edgar had written to one of his creditors, "I have tried to get the money for you from Mr. A[llan] a dozen times—but he always shuffles me off. . . . Mr. A is not often very sober—which accounts for it."[3]

The creditor showed Allan the letter. Allan was furious because Edgar had slandered him by saying that he was an alcoholic. He demanded an explanation. Poe made matters even worse. He said that the accusation was true. He also blamed Allan for all his problems because Allan had cut his financial support. That was the last straw. Allan cut him off completely. Once again Edgar had lost both his father and his mother.

At West Point, he stopped going to formations. He began cutting classes. He refused to obey orders. In early 1831, less than a year after entering West Point, Edgar was court-martialed and dismissed from the academy. He sailed down the Hudson River to New York City, where he found a small publisher for his third book, *Poems by Edgar A. Poe.* Then he moved to Baltimore, where he lived with his aunt, Maria Poe Clemm, and his young cousin Virginia. He also spent time with his brother Henry, but that reunion was short-lived: Henry died that fall.

Soon afterward, Poe entered a magazine contest. Though he didn't win the cash prize, the magazine published his story "Metzengerstein" and several others. While it must have been encouraging to see his stories in print, he was virtually destitute. His aunt's wages as a dressmaker barely supported the three of them. Edgar helped out by tutoring Virginia. He wrote a letter to Allan, begging for money. It was ignored.

Hearing in 1834 that John Allan was dying, Edgar paid him one last visit. Allan roused enough strength to threaten him with a cane. When he died a few weeks later, Edgar attended the reading of the will. Allan had been successful in his relationship with his new wife. He finally had children of his own. Edgar learned that he wouldn't receive anything from the estate. By this time, Poe was suffering from depression. He was also drinking heavily.

Soon after Allan's death, it seemed as if Poe's luck might be about to change. American cities were thriving. There was a corresponding rise in the demand for public education and for reading materials. A novelist named John Pendleton Kennedy became a mentor for Poe. He put him in touch with Thomas W. White, who had founded a magazine called *Southern Literary Messenger.*

White printed some of Poe's work. Then he asked Poe to come to Richmond and work with him on the magazine. Professionally, it was a good move. Personally, it was not. He had to leave his aunt and cousin. They were all the family he had left. As would soon be obvious, Edgar thought of "family" in more than one way.

Maria sent him a very upsetting letter. Neilson Poe, a well-to-do cousin who lived in Maryland, had offered to take Virginia into his home, and quite likely Maria as well. Poe was devastated. "It is useless to disguise the truth that when Virginia goes with N. P. that I shall never behold her again—that is absolutely sure," he wrote to Maria. "Pity me, my dear Aunty, pity me, I have no one now to fly to."[4] He made a counteroffer: come to Richmond to live with him. Maria agreed. On the way to Baltimore to get them, he picked up a marriage license. Edgar Allan Poe was one of the names that appeared on the document. Virginia Clemm was the other. He was twenty-six. She was thirteen.

FYInfo

The United States Military Academy

The United States Military Academy is more familiarly known as West Point. The nickname comes from the academy's location—a bluff overlooking a bend in the Hudson River about fifty miles north of New York City. It opened its doors on July 4, 1802.

West Point served as a fort during the Revolutionary War. When the war was over, George Washington and many citizens of the newly established country agreed they needed an institution to provide formal training for army officers. Finally, when Thomas Jefferson became president, legislation to establish the academy was enacted.

The school began to achieve its present reputation as an elite institution when Colonel Sylvanus Thayer became superintendent in 1817. Known as "the father of the Military Academy," he served for the next sixteen years and established the strong sense of discipline and academic accomplishment that still characterize West Point. He also laid the groundwork for what would become the academy's motto: "Duty, Honor, Country." Poe arrived at West Point—and left—during Thayer's tenure.

The Civil War forced a difficult choice on many graduates. They had taken an oath to support the Union when they received their commissions, but their home states had seceded. Generals such as Robert E. Lee, Stonewall Jackson, and Jeb Stuart fought for the

General Robert E. Lee

Confederacy, while Jefferson Davis served as its president. Ulysses S. Grant and William Tecumseh Sherman, the two most famous Union generals, were also West Point graduates.

Grant and fellow West Pointer Dwight D. Eisenhower achieved the nation's highest political office when each was elected president (Grant served from 1869 to 1877; Eisenhower, 1953 to 1961). Another academy graduate, Abner Doubleday, achieved distinction in a very different field—he is generally given credit for inventing the game of baseball.

Women were admitted to West Point for the first time in 1976. They currently compose 15 percent of the Corps of Cadets, which numbers about 4,000. All cadets are commissioned as second lieutenants when they graduate. They are required to serve for at least five years in active duty and three years in the reserves.

Some art historians believe that this painting by Thomas Sully depicts Virginia Clemm Poe. Born in 1783, Sully came to the United States as a child. He became one of the country's most famous painters. He was especially noted for his portraits of women. He died in 1872.

Chapter 4

A SEA STORY

Poe married Virginia several months later. He, his new bride, and his aunt (who was also now his mother-in-law) all moved into a boardinghouse in Richmond. Life continued to be a struggle. Poe began working feverishly, writing stories, essays, poems, and reviews of the work of other authors. The circulation of the magazine began to increase, and Poe's reviews were one of the main reasons. Some were kind, but the majority were very critical. Sometimes the authors he attacked would write letters attacking him. The public loved the hostile interchanges and eagerly bought the magazine to read them.

Meanwhile Poe was drinking again, and drinking way too much. He was also unhappy with White. He didn't believe that he was getting enough credit for the success of the magazine. Early in 1837 White couldn't put up with him any longer and fired him.

Poe received an offer to go to New York City and work on the *New York Review*. The job fell through. During this time, he worked on what would become by far his longest story, *The Narrative of Arthur Gordon Pym of Nantucket*.

The story was inspired by events in the world around him. In 1836, an ambitious man named Jeremiah Reynolds had urged the U.S. government to undertake a scientific expedition to the South Seas, and in particular to the almost unknown continent of Antarctica and perhaps even to the South Pole itself. His efforts resulted in a great deal of publicity and would eventually result in the formation of the United States South Seas Exploring Expedition.

Very little was known of Antarctica. That was fine with Poe. He wanted to use the mysterious continent as a backdrop for what became a combination sea story—a popular form of literature—and his growing interest in writing horror. The story contains murder, butchery, massacres, shipwrecks, starvation, a number of near-death experiences, and other events that reflected the turmoil in Poe's own mind.

Severe financial turmoil in the United States—the Panic of 1837—not only deferred *Pym*'s publication but also made it very difficult for Poe to find steady work. The family moved to Philadelphia the following year, and *Pym* was finally published. It did not sell well.

In 1839, Poe met William Burton, who had started *Burton's Gentleman's Magazine.* Burton hired Poe, but he couldn't afford to pay him very much. Poe still continued to work hard. That fall he published one his most famous stories, "The Fall of the House of Usher." It includes elements of terror and supernatural events that characterize much of his work. The story's narrator visits his friend Roderick Usher, a gloomy man who lives in an equally gloomy house with his sister Madeline. During the visit, Madeline dies. The narrator and Roderick carry the coffin into the family vault in the cellar. One stormy night not long afterward, the two men hear a strange noise. To their horror, they find it is Madeline. She had been buried alive but somehow managed to claw her way out of the coffin. Nearly dead, she seeks out Roderick and grabs him. Horror-stricken,

This photograph of Antarctica reveals its harsh conditions. Even in summer, temperatures are just above freezing. There is almost no vegetation. In winter, the ice forms a solid barrier and the sun disappears for several weeks.

he dies at the same moment as his sister. The narrator flees and the house collapses into a swamp.

Even though a publisher printed a collection of his short stories called *Tales of the Grotesque and Arabesque,* Poe felt that he wasn't being appreciated. He regarded his routine duties at the magazine as a waste of time. He tried to start his own magazine, but the country was still having financial troubles. Few people had the money or the inclination to invest in what seemed to be a fairly shaky venture. Potential subscribers also shied away. Early in 1841, Poe abandoned the idea.

In the meantime, George Rex Graham had purchased Burton's magazine and retitled it *Graham's Magazine*. One of its first stories was "The Murders in the Rue Morgue." Graham published other articles and stories by Poe. The magazine's circulation began climbing rapidly. It appeared that Poe was about to achieve the success and personal happiness for which he had worked so long and so hard.

FYInfo

The Ex. Ex.

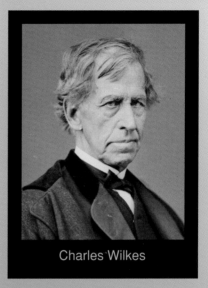

Charles Wilkes

Generated by Jeremiah Reynolds's passionate appeal to Congress, the United States South Seas Exploring Expedition was a bold venture for a country that had been in existence for only a few decades. The Ex. Ex., as it quickly became known, left Norfolk, Virginia, in August 1838. Consisting of six ships and 346 seamen, it was commanded by Lieutenant Charles Wilkes, the head of the U.S. Navy's Department of Charts and Instruments. Wilkes, who had little actual sea experience, acquired a reputation as a harsh disciplinarian. So harsh, in fact, that he was court-martialed and received a letter of reprimand when the expedition returned to New York in June 1842.

During its voyage, the Ex. Ex. covered more than 87,000 miles. It was the final all-sail naval expedition to circumnavigate the earth. Although two ships and twenty-eight men were lost, the venture was considered a success. Wilkes, with seven scientists and two artists, compiled a great deal of information. The expedition made major contributions in the fields of geography, botany, zoology, and anthropology. It was responsible for mapping hundreds of miles of previously unexplored Antarctic coastline. The men visited nearly 300 islands in the Pacific Ocean, most notably Fiji

and Hawaii. They also sailed to what are now Washington and Oregon and returned with charts of those areas. It was the first major American expedition to that region since the time of Lewis and Clark, nearly forty years earlier. The Ex. Ex. returned with tens of thousands of specimens of birds, sea life, and plants from all the different locations they had explored.

Except for when he served in the Civil War (during which he was court-martialed again), Wilkes spent most of the rest of his life working on reports of the expedition. The materials he brought back formed the basis for the foundation of the Smithsonian Institution in Washington, D.C. Part of Antarctica is named Wilkes Land, honoring the explorer who first sighted it.

This image shows the Poe Cottage in The Bronx, New York. It was Poe's final home. He lived there from 1846 to 1849. Today the Poe Cottage is a museum that is open to the public. Visitors can see Poe's rocking chair and the bed where his wife Virginia died.

Chapter 5

A MYSTERIOUS END

In the summer of 1841, Poe wrote a short story called "Eleonora," which had a number of autobiographical elements. It was about a young man who marries his cousin, but the cousin dies. The story proved to be eerily prophetic.

One evening early the following year, the Poes had some friends over for a relaxing evening. Virginia began to entertain everyone by singing. She had a clear voice and people enjoyed listening to her. Suddenly she stopped singing. She doubled over in agony, with a severe fit of coughing. A blood vessel in her lungs had burst. Some historians have speculated that one of the reasons Edgar had been so attracted to Virginia was that she looked so much like his memories of his mother. Unfortunately, the coughing fit was yet another way in which Virginia resembled the dead Elizabeth. She had contracted tuberculosis. She would never be the same. After the blood vessel burst, she required constant care and attention. Poe became frantic at the thought of her death.

Poe's depression surfaced at work. As always, he believed that he wasn't being paid enough. He also began arguing with other people on the magazine staff. Finally he had enough. He walked away, never to return.

He made a trip to Washington, D.C., to ask the new president, John Tyler, for a government job working in a customs house. If he had been successful, it would have been a huge help. Another contemporary writer, Nathaniel Hawthorne, held two customs house jobs during the years he was becoming established. Poe wasn't as fortunate. Even though he was a good friend of Tyler's son Robert, he didn't get the job.

Poe continued writing. In June 1843, he received a rare dose of good news. His short story "The Gold-Bug" won a prize of one hundred dollars. It also brought him a great deal of fame when it was published. It is one of his most famous stories.

Later that year, he began working on a new poem. It is about a man who has unhappy memories of his lost love. Entitled "The Raven," it begins,

> "Once upon a midnight dreary, while I pondered, weak and weary . . . "

A raven flies into the man's room. The man asks the bird a series of questions, but it can only answer with a single word: *Nevermore.* The poem concludes as the narrator realizes that his soul will "nevermore" be freed from the shadow of his former love.

The employees at *Graham's Magazine,* where he first submitted "The Raven," were disappointed. They didn't like the poem and rejected it. When Poe moved to New York City with Virginia and Maria, he submitted it to the *New York Mirror.* When they printed it early in 1845, the poem created a sensation. It was reprinted in newspapers all over the country.

However, its popularity didn't translate into financial success for its author. Poe continued to struggle to make enough money to support his family. Coupled with the anguish of Virginia's continuing illness, it drove Poe to depression and self-destructive drinking. He became jealous of writers who earned more money than he did. In a search for some peace and cleaner surroundings, he moved to a cottage outside the city in the spring of 1846.

By then he had achieved some success in a new career: public speaking. In an era when there were few forms of popular entertainment, people enjoyed going to public lectures. The benefit was more than intellectual. The lectures also offered the chance for people to get out of their houses and mingle with friends and neighbors. Poe's reputation as a somewhat odd author worked in his favor. People were especially interested in listening to him.

But the money he earned wasn't enough to save Virginia. She died early in 1847. Edgar was so depressed and despondent that he hardly ever left the house. Maria Clemm raised a little money by begging. Slowly he recovered.

Desperately craving the companionship that Virginia had given him, Poe found another outlet for his affections in the fall of 1848. He renewed a brief acquaintance with a woman named Sarah Helen Whitman. He proposed marriage two days later—in a cemetery. She turned him down, saying that she was too old for him (forty-five to his thirty-nine) and that her health wasn't good enough. Poe persisted, and Sarah finally changed her mind. On the eve of the ceremony, she learned how much he drank. She turned him down again.

While the fiasco embarrassed him, he still wanted to start a new literary magazine. He traveled to numerous cities, giving lectures about his stories and theories of writing in an effort to raise money for it. In July 1849, he was back in Richmond. He was reunited with Elmira Royster Shelton, his childhood sweetheart. Her husband had died and the two quickly rekindled the affection they had had for each other more than two decades earlier. She set down one condition. Poe had to join the Sons of Temperance, an anti-alcohol group. He agreed. He sent enthusiastic letters to Maria Clemm, expressing happiness with his situation.

"I never was received with so much enthusiasm," he wrote after one of his lectures. "The papers have done nothing but praise me."[1] A few weeks later, after spending an evening with Elmira, he sent Maria another letter. "I think she loves me more devotedly than any one I ever knew and I cannot help loving her in return."[2]

Fortune finally seemed to be smiling on Edgar Allan Poe. He was in love, his lectures were popular and well paying, and he had given up drinking alcohol.

On September 27, 1849, he boarded a boat in Richmond. His itinerary was precise. He would sail to Baltimore, catch a train to Philadelphia for a business appointment, then continue to New York to pick up Maria Clemm. The two of them would return to Richmond for the wedding.

Poe never made it to New York. There is no reliable explanation for what happened during the days after he got off the boat in Baltimore. Perhaps he went on a drinking binge. Because Baltimore was in the midst of an election campaign, he may have fallen victim to roving gangs that rounded up men on the street, kept them in an alcoholic stupor, then carried them from polling place to polling place so that they could "vote early and vote often." There is also speculation that Elmira's brothers may have beaten him up because they didn't want a man with a dubious reputation marrying their sister. Some scholars have theorized that he succumbed to a serious illness; a brain tumor and a diabetic coma are among the possibilities that have been mentioned.

What is known is that a printer named Joseph Walker found Poe lying just outside a tavern on the afternoon of October 3. Poe was barely conscious and wearing dirty, cast-off clothing—much different from the elegant apparel he had been wearing when he left Richmond. He asked Walker to locate his friend Joseph Snodgrass. When the worried Snodgrass arrived, he took Poe to the hospital.

For several days, Poe barely clung to life, alternating between periods of unconsciousness and delirious outbursts. Early on the morning of October 7, he whispered, "Lord help my poor soul."[3] Moments later, he was dead.

According to several sources, Poe repeatedly called out the name Reynolds in the final hours of his life. It is possible he was calling the same Jeremiah Reynolds who had advocated the expedition to Antarctica and had been the primary inspiration for *The Narrative of Arthur Gordon Pym*.

As *Pym* concludes, the boat bearing Pym and one other crew member is rushing toward a cataract, or waterfall, in Antarctica. "We rushed into the embraces of the cataract, where a chasm threw itself open to receive us," Poe writes. "But there arose in our pathway a shrouded human figure, very far larger in its proportions than any dweller among men. And the hue of the skin of the figure was of the perfect whiteness of the snow."[4]

Since the book is dotted with references to Poe's family, the shrouded figure could well have been Poe's mother. In his final agony, he may have remembered the pallor of her skin when he was a toddler. She certainly would have seemed a larger-than-life figure to him at that time. Nearly four decades later, he was finally reunited with her in death.

Much of Edgar Allan Poe's life had been a tortured search for motherly warmth and security. Now he was finally at peace.

His reputation wasn't. The trusting Maria Clemm gave her dead son-in-law's stories and other writings to an editor named Rufus Griswold. It was a serious error in judgment. Poe had savagely attacked Griswold several years earlier. Griswold had an inflated opinion of his writing ability, and he deeply resented the attacks. But he didn't do anything while Poe was still alive. Once Poe was dead, Griswold had his chance for revenge. He published the material that Maria Clemm had given him. He also published a biography that was filled with distortions and outright lies about Poe. This biography colored people's opinions of Poe for many years.

Gradually the picture became clearer. Today Poe is recognized as one of this country's most important writers. Poems such as "The Raven" and his many short stories remain very popular. Countless numbers of people enjoy reading them. Some of his stories have been made into movies. Others are featured in television productions. He is also the icon of the group Mystery Writers of America, who confer the Edgar Allan Poe Awards (the Edgars) in a number of categories at a gala annual banquet.

Edgar Allan Poe may have lived much of his life in poverty. He left a literary legacy that is among the richest in all of American literature.

In 1949—the centennial of his death—another type of legacy began. Shortly after midnight on January 19—Poe's birthday—a man wearing a black hat and white scarf that obscured his face visited the cemetery where Poe is buried. He placed three roses and half a bottle of cognac on the tombstone. Every year after that, the enigmatic figure has reappeared on January 19 in the dark early morning hours.

There may have been a change in 1993. That year, the secret visitor left a note saying, "The torch will be passed."[5] It is believed that the man's sons have taken over the responsibility, as a later note said that the original visitor died in 1998. If that is true, the man took his identity to his grave.

It is a fitting memorial to the man who invented the mystery story.

FYInfo

Nathaniel Hawthorne

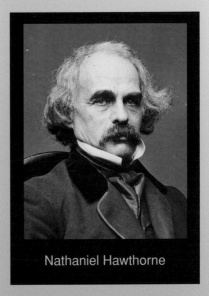

Nathaniel Hawthorne

Nathaniel Hawthorne was born on July 4, 1804, in Salem, Massachusetts. His ancestors included John Hathorne, one of the presiding judges in the notorious Salem witch trials of 1692. His father was a ship's captain who died at sea when Nathaniel was only four. His mother became very protective of her son and raised him in seclusion.

He entered Bowdoin College in Maine when he was seventeen. His classmates and friends included poet Henry Wadsworth Longfellow and Franklin Pierce, a future president of the United States. After he graduated in 1825, he returned to his mother's house. He lived there for twelve years, writing a number of short stories and reading a great deal. He collected some of these stories in 1837 and published them in a book entitled *Twice-Told Tales,* which Poe reviewed—not altogether favorably.

Hawthorne didn't make very much money from his writing. He obtained a political appointment in the Boston Customs House in 1839 in order to earn enough money to marry a woman named Sophia Peabody. After their wedding three years later, the couple moved to nearby Concord. Their neighbors included Ralph Waldo Emerson and Henry David Thoreau.

Hawthorne took another customs house job in 1846, this time in Salem.

In 1850, he published his most famous novel, *The Scarlet Letter.* It is considered to be one of the classic works in the history of American literature. *The House of the Seven Gables* (1851) and *The Blithedale Romance* (1852) quickly followed.

In 1853, his friend Franklin Pierce was elected president. Pierce appointed Hawthorne to the position of United States consul in Liverpool, England. He remained there for four years until Pierce left office. Hawthorne toured Europe for the following two years and published his final novel, *The Marble Faun,* when he returned to the United States in 1860.

He died on May 19, 1864, in Plymouth, New Hampshire.

CHRONOLOGY

1809	Born on January 19 in Boston, Massachusetts
1810	Father leaves and presumably dies
1811	Mother dies; Edgar adopted by John and Frances Allan
1815	Moves with the Allans to England
1820	Returns to United States
1826	Enters the University of Virginia
1827	Enlists in U.S. Army; publishes *Tamerlane and Other Poems*
1830	Enters the U.S. Military Academy at West Point
1831	Expelled from West Point; moves to Baltimore and lives with his aunt Maria Clemm and his cousin Virginia
1835	Begins writing for *Southern Literary Messenger*
1836	Marries Virginia Clemm
1837	Moves to New York
1838	Moves to Philadelphia; publishes *The Narrative of Arthur Gordon Pym of Nantucket*
1839	Writes for *Burton's Gentleman's Magazine;* publishes "The Fall of the House of Usher"
1840	*Tales of the Grotesque and Arabesque,* his first collection of short stories, is published
1841	Works for *Graham's Magazine;* publishes "The Murders in the Rue Morgue"
1843	Publishes "The Gold-Bug"
1845	Moves to New York; publishes "The Raven"
1847	Wife, Virginia, dies
1849	Dies on October 7 in Baltimore, Maryland

SELECTED WORKS

Poems

1845	"The Raven"
1849	"Annabel Lee"
1849	"The Bells"
1849	"Eldorado"

Short Stories

1833	"MS. Found in a Bottle"
1838	"Ligeia"
1839	"The Fall of the House of Usher"
1839	"William Wilson"
1841	"The Murders in the Rue Morgue"
1842	"The Mystery of Marie Rogêt"
1842	"The Masque of the Red Death"
1842	"The Pit and the Pendulum"
1843	"The Gold-Bug"
1843	"The Black Cat"
1843	"The Tell-Tale Heart"
1845	"The Facts in the Case of M. Valdemar"
1846	"The Cask of Amontillado"
1846	"Hop-Frog"

Novel

1838	*The Narrative of Arthur Gordon Pym of Nantucket*

TIMELINE IN HISTORY

1729 The city of Baltimore, Maryland, is founded.

1743 Thomas Jefferson, who will write the Declaration of Independence and become the third U.S. president, is born.

1752 Benjamin Franklin flies a kite during a severe storm, proving that lightning is electricity.

1756 The Seven Years' War between England and France for control of the American colonies begins.

1775 The battles of Lexington and Concord begin the Revolutionary War.

1783 U.S. author Washington Irving is born; his short stories will include "Rip Van Winkle" and "The Legend of Sleepy Hollow."

1793 Construction of the U.S. Capitol building in Washington, D.C., begins.

1802 The U.S. Military Academy at West Point is founded.

1804 U.S. author Nathaniel Hawthorne is born.

1809 U.S. president Abraham Lincoln is born.

1811 U.S. author Harriet Beecher Stowe, who will write *Uncle Tom's Cabin*, is born.

1812 The War of 1812 begins.

1814 Francis Scott Key writes "The Star-Spangled Banner" at Fort McHenry in Baltimore.

1820 The Missouri Compromise allows Maine to enter the Union as a free state and Missouri to enter as a slave state.

1826 John Adams and Thomas Jefferson, former presidents and signers of the Declaration of Independence, die on July 4, the document's fiftieth anniversary.

1828 Andrew Jackson becomes U.S. president.

1831 French author Victor Hugo writes *The Hunchback of Notre Dame*.

1837 The Panic of 1837 results in economic depression in the United States.

1838 U.S. South Seas Exploring Expedition departs; it returns nearly four years later.

1844 The first telegraph message is sent.

1848 Gold is discovered in California, leading to a westward rush of gold seekers the following year.

1851 U.S. author Herman Melville publishes *Moby Dick*.

1860 Abraham Lincoln wins U.S. presidential election.

1861 Led by South Carolina, Southern states secede and form the Confederate States of America.

TIMELINE IN HISTORY (CONT'D)

1862 Lincoln signs the Emancipation Proclamation, which frees all slaves as of January 1, 1863.

1868 Wilkie Collins publishes *The Moonstone,* developing the characteristics of modern detective novels.

1879 Thomas Edison invents the electric light.

1883 William F. "Buffalo Bill" Cody organizes his Wild West Show.

1887 Sir Arthur Conan Doyle publishes his first Sherlock Holmes mystery, *A Study in Scarlet.*

1895 U.S. author Stephen Crane publishes *The Red Badge of Courage.*

1900 English author Beatrix Potter publishes *Peter Rabbit.*

1920 Agatha Christie publishes her first novel, *The Mysterious Affair at Styles*, which is also the first to feature Hercule Poirot.

2005 *Chasing Vermeer* by Blue Balliett wins "Edgar" for best Juvenile Mystery Novel

GLOSSARY

aristocrat
(ah-RIS-tuh-krat)—a member of the privileged class.

boardinghouse
(BOR-ding-HOUSE)—a place that rents rooms and provides meals for its guests.

circulation
(sir-kyoo-LAY-shun)—for newspapers or magazines, the number of copies sold of each edition.

circumnavigate
(sir-kum-NAA-vih-gate)—to travel entirely around.

cognac
(KUNH-yak)—a brown alcoholic beverage that is made in France.

court-martialed
(KORT mar-shuld)—brought up on charges in a military court, usually consisting of commissioned officers.

customs house
(KUSS-tums HOUSE)—a building, usually located in a port city, in which officials collect taxes and duties on goods coming into the country.

fiasco
(fee-ASS-koe)—a complete and total failure.

precocious
(prih-KOE-shuss)—showing a high degree of intelligence or maturity at an early age.

tithe—to give ten percent of one's income.

FURTHER READING

For Young Adults

Kent, Zachary. *Edgar Allan Poe: Tragic Poet and Master of Mystery.* Berkeley Heights, N.J.: Enslow Publishers, 2001.

Meltzer, Milton. *Edgar Allan Poe: A Biography.* Brookfield, Conn.: Twenty-First Century Books, 2003.

Peltak, Jennifer. *Edgar Allan Poe (Who Wrote That?).* Langhorne, Penn.: Chelsea House Publishers, 2004.

Schoell, William. *Mystery and Terror: The Story of Edgar Allan Poe.* Greensboro, N.C.: Morgan Reynolds, 2004.

Streissguth, Tom. *Edgar Allan Poe.* Minneapolis: Lerner Publications Company, 2001.

Tilton, Rafael. *The Importance of Edgar Allan Poe.* San Diego: Lucent Books, 2001.

Works Consulted

Kennedy, J. Gerald (editor). *A Historical Guide to Edgar Allan Poe.* New York: Oxford University Press, 2001.

Mankowitz, Wolf. *The Extraordinary Mr. Poe.* London: Weidenfeld and Nicolson, 1978.

Meyers, Jeffrey. *Edgar Allan Poe.* New York: Macmillan Publishing Company, 1992.

Poe, Edgar Allan. *The Narrative of Arthur Gordon Pym of Nantucket.* New York: Penguin Books, 1999.

———. *Thirty-Two Stories.* Edited by Stuart Levine and Susan F. Levine. Indianapolis: Hackett Publishing Company, 2000.

Silverman, Kenneth. *Edgar A. Poe: Mournful and Never-Ending Remembrance.* New York: HarperCollins Publishers, 1991.

Sinclair, David. *Edgar Allan Poe.* London: J.M. Dent & Sons, 1977.

On the Internet

The Edgar Allan Poe Society of Baltimore
    http://www.eapoe.org/

An In-depth Look at Edgar Allan Poe
    http://empirezine.com/spotlight/poe/poe1.htm

The Murder of Edgar Allan Poe
    http://www.crimelibrary.com/notorious_murders/celebrity/edgar_allan_poe/

Poe Museum
    http://www.poemuseum.org/

"Poe and Griswold"
    http://www.eapoe.org/geninfo/poegrisw.htm

Doyle, Arthur Conan. *Through the Magic Door,*
    http://www.classic-literature.co.uk/scottish-authors/arthur-conan-doyle/
    through-the-magic-door/index.asp

History of Tuberculosis
    http://www.goshen.edu/bio/Biol206/Biol206LabProject/tricia/Tbhx.html

MacGowan, Douglass. "The Murder Mystery of Mary Rogers."
    http://www.crimelibrary.com/notorious_murders/classics/mary_rogers/
    index.html?sect=13

FURTHER READING (CONT'D)

Nathaniel Hawthorne
http://www.bedfordstmartins.com/literature/bedlit/authors_depth/
hawthorne.htm
New Jersey's History's Mysteries: "Mary Cecilea Rogers and the Legend of Sybil's
Cave,"
http://www.njhm.com/maryrogers.htm
United States Exploring Expedition, 1838–1842
http://www.sil.si.edu/DigitalCollections/usexex/learn/Philbrick.htm
USMA Bicentennial Celebration
http://www.usma.edu/bicentennial/history/Preface.asp

CHAPTER NOTES

Chapter 1
A Gruesome Crime
1. Arthur Conan Doyle, *Through the Magic Door,* http://www.classic-literature.co.uk/scottish-authors/arthur-conan-doyle/through-the-magic-door/index.asp, p. 27.

Chapter 2
Acting Out His Part
1. Wolf Mankowitz, *The Extraordinary Mr. Poe* (London: Weidenfeld and Nicolson, 1978), p. 17.
2. Jeffrey Meyers, *Edgar Allan Poe* (New York: Macmillan Publishing Company, 1992), p. 9.
3. David Sinclair, *Edgar Allan Poe* (London: J.M. Dent & Sons, 1977), p. 48.
4. Kenneth Silverman, *Edgar A. Poe: Mournful and Never-Ending Remembrance* (New York: HarperCollins Publishers, 1991), p. 27.

Chapter 3
Cadet Poe
1. Jeffrey Meyers, *Edgar Allan Poe* (New York: Macmillan Publishing Company, 1992), p. 29.

2. *Antiques Road Show FYI:* "Missing Masterpieces," http://www.pbs.org/wgbh/antiquesfyi/missingmasterpieces/
3. Meyers, p. 48.
4. Kenneth Silverman, *Edgar A. Poe: Mournful and Never-Ending Remembrance* (New York: HarperCollins Publishers, 1991), p. 104.

Chapter 5
A Mysterious End
1. David Sinclair, *Edgar Allan Poe* (London: J.M. Dent & Sons, 1977), pp. 249–50.
2. Ibid., p. 251.
3. Wolf Mankowitz, *The Extraordinary Mr. Poe* (London: Weidenfeld and Nicolson, 1978), p. 242.
4. Edgar Allan Poe, *The Narrative of Arthur Gordon Pym of Nantucket* (New York: Penguin Books, 1999), p. 217.
5. Kasey Jones, "Mysterious Fan Marks Poe's Birthday," *Seattle Post-Intelligencer,* January 19, 2005.

INDEX